Spring Ha
Bible Workbook

LETTERS TO THE CHURCHES

LIFESTYLE

SPRING
HARVEST
Equipping the Church for action

First published in 2002 by Spring Harvest Publishing Division and Authentic Lifestyle

07 06 05 04 03 02 01   7 6 5 4 3 2 01

Authentic Lifestyle is an imprint of Authentic Media
PO Box 300, Carlisle, Cumbria, CA3 0QS, UK
and
Box 1047, Waynesboro, GA 30830-2047, USA
www.paternoster-publishing.com

British Library Cataloguing in Publication Data

A catalogue record for this book is available from the British Library

ISBN 1-85078-441-8

Typeset by Spring Harvest
Printed in Great Britain by Bell and Bain Ltd., Glasgow

CONTENTS

ABOUT THIS BOOK

This study book looks at the letters to the seven churches in the first three chapters of Revelation, and considers their relevance to us. Rather than a verse-by-verse exposition, this guide picks out themes and looks at some of the letters together.

This book is written primarily for a group situation, but can easily be used by individuals who want to study the issues it covers. It can be used in a variety of contexts, so it is perhaps helpful to spell out the assumptions that we have made about the groups that will use it. Groups can have a variety of names – homegroups, Bible study groups, cell groups – we've used housegroup as the generic term.

▶ The emphasis of the studies will be on the application of the Bible. Group members will not just learn facts, but will be encouraged to think 'How does this apply to me? What change does it require of me? What incidents or situations in my life is this relevant to?'
▶ Housegroups can encourage honesty and make space for questions and doubts. The aim of the studies is not to find the 'right answer', but to help members understand the Bible by working through their questions. The Christian faith often throws up paradoxes. Events in people's lives may make particular verses difficult to understand or believe. The housegroup should be a safe place to express these concerns.
▶ Housegroups can give opportunities for deep friendships to develop. Group members will be encouraged to talk about their experiences, feelings, questions, hopes and fears. They will be able to offer one another pastoral support and to get involved in each others' lives.
▶ There is a difference between being a collection of individuals who happen to meet together every Wednesday and an effective group who bounce ideas off each other, spark inspiration and creativity, pool their talents and resources to create solutions together and whose whole is definitely greater than the sum of its parts. The process of working through these studies will encourage healthy group dynamics.

Space is given for you to write answers, comments, questions and thoughts. This book will not tell you what to think, but will help you to discover the truth of God's word through thinking, discussing, praying and listening.

FOR GROUP MEMBERS

▶ You will probably get more out of the study if you spend some time during the week reading the passage and thinking about the questions. Make a note of anything you don't understand.

▶ Pray that God will help you to understand the passage and show you how to apply it. Pray for other members in your group too, that they will find the study helpful.

▶ Be willing to take part in the discussions. The leader of the group is not there as the expert with all the answers. They will want everyone to get involved and share thoughts and opinions.

▶ However, don't dominate the group! If you are aware that you are saying a lot, make space for other people to contribute. Be sensitive to other group members and aim to be encouraging. If you disagree with someone, say so without putting down their contribution.

FOR INDIVIDUALS

▶ Although this book is written with a group in mind, it can also be easily used by individuals. You obviously won't be able to do the group activities suggested, but you can consider how you would answer the questions and write your thoughts in the space provided.

▶ You may find it helpful to talk to a prayer partner about what you have learned, and ask them to pray for you as you try to apply what you are reading to your life.

▶ The New International Version of the text is printed in the book. If you usually use a different version, then read from your own Bible as well.

INTRODUCTION TO
LETTERS TO THE CHURCHES

Imagine that you are a follower of Jesus and a member of the only Christian church in your city. Your nearest neighbouring church is over forty miles away and there is no easy transport system linking the two. There are no opportunities to meet together, Spring Harvest style, for teaching and encouragement, no Christian books, no New Testament. The leader who has been very significant to your church has been threatened, tortured and deported.

You have lived through a turbulent time – earthquakes have shaken the land you live in, political uprisings have resulted in unprecedented bloodshed. Everyone is very tense about the future, wondering what will happen next.

You and your church are under threat. You worry that your neighbours will report you to the authorities for being an 'atheist', as they call you. The city that you live in is a place where occultism and paganism thrive. The national political leader is feeling insecure and is talking about loyalty to him and to the state being the only acceptable form of worship. Some fellow Christians have turned away from the faith because of the pressure. You thought that Jesus was going to return soon and impose his kingdom rule on all the chaos around you – but you are still waiting.

The seven churches in Asia found themselves in a very similar situation towards the end of the first century. And then came the good news – they had mail. Their beloved leader John had written words received from Jesus himself, words of encouragement, rebuke, challenge and hope.

It's easy to see Revelation as an impenetrable book of apocalyptic visions. In fact it was written for a church stuck in the gap between promise and fulfilment. It was written to people who needed a fresh vision of Christ. It was a call to genuine discipleship in the face of great pressure. It shows us some of what Christ thinks of his church – what brings a smile to his face and what angers him. And even though it was written nearly two thousand years ago, we will find as we study it that it is still relevant to our situation today. We've got mail too.

YOU'VE GOT MAIL – THE CHURCH UNDER PRESSURE

AIM: to introduce the book of Revelation

The revelation of Jesus Christ, which God gave him to show his servants what must soon take place. He made it known by sending his angel to his servant John, who testifies to everything he saw – that is, the word of God and the testimony of Jesus Christ. Blessed is the one who reads the words of this prophecy, and blessed are those who hear it and take to heart what is written in it, because the time is near.

John,

To the seven churches in the province of Asia:

Grace and peace to you from him who is, and who was, and who is to come, and from the seven spirits before his throne, and from Jesus Christ, who is the faithful witness, the firstborn from the dead, and the ruler of the kings of the earth.

To him who loves us and has freed us from our sins by his blood, and has made us to be a kingdom and priests to serve his God and Father – to him be glory and power for ever and ever! Amen.

Look, he is coming with the clouds,
and every eye will see him,
even those who pierced him;
and all the peoples of the earth will mourn because of him.
So shall it be! Amen.

"I am the Alpha and the Omega," says the Lord God, "who is, and who was, and who is to come, the Almighty."

I, John, your brother and companion in the suffering and kingdom and patient endurance that are ours in Jesus, was on the island of Patmos because of the word of God and the testimony of Jesus. On the Lord's Day I was in the Spirit, and I heard behind me a loud voice like a trumpet, which said: "Write on a scroll what you see and send it to the seven churches: to Ephesus, Smyrna, Pergamum, Thyatira, Sardis, Philadelphia and Laodicea."

I turned around to see the voice that was speaking to me. And when I turned I saw seven golden lampstands, and among the lampstands was someone "like a son of man", dressed in a robe reaching down to his feet and with a golden sash around his chest. His head and hair were white like wool, as white as snow, and his eyes were like blazing fire. His feet were like bronze glowing in a furnace, and his voice was like the sound of rushing waters. In his right hand he held seven stars, and out of his mouth came a sharp double-edged sword. His face was like the sun shining in all its brilliance.

When I saw him, I fell at his feet as though dead. Then he placed his right hand on me and said: "Do not be afraid. I am the First and the Last. I am the Living One; I was dead, and behold I am alive for ever and ever! And I hold the keys of death and Hades.

"Write, therefore, what you have seen, what is now and what will take place later. The mystery of the seven stars that you saw in my right hand and of the seven golden lampstands is this: The seven stars are the angels of the seven churches, and the seven lampstands are the seven churches."

Revelation 1:1-20

TO SET THE SCENE
How good are you at solving crosswords? Have a go while you drink your coffee!

Read Revelation 1:1-20

HOW DOES THIS / APPLY TO ME

1   Discuss how you feel about the book of Revelation. If it were a film, what kind of film would it be? If it were a piece of mail sent through the post, what would it be?

WHAT DOES / SEARCH / THE BIBLE SAY?

2   Who is Revelation about (v1)? What will happen to those who read it and take to heart these words (v3)? Originally written to specific churches in a specific context, these words of Jesus concerning how he wants his church to be are eternally relevant to us too.

APPLY THIS TO / MY CHURCH

3   Read the Churches under pressure box to find out about the churches that this letter was originally written to, and the world they lived in. What similarities and differences are there between these churches and your church today?

HOW DOES THIS / APPLY TO ME

4   What pressures do you feel under personally?

5   Jesus gave a fresh vision of himself to the seven churches. From these verses, pick out the reminders of who he is and what he has done.

6   Verse 1 talks about what must soon take place, verse 3 says that the time is near – and yet we are still waiting for the Second Coming. How should we understand the words 'soon' and 'near'?

APPLY THIS TO / MY CHURCH

7   As we look at these letters to the seven churches, we will be applying the words to our own church. Write a 'code of conduct' for how you would like to discuss your own church.

'Christians down the years have fondly assumed that churches are automatically on the side of God, and he is on their side. The letters of Revelation show this to be a dangerous delusion.'

Stephen Travis

Churches under pressure

▶ The seven churches were scattered over a wide area in modern-day western Turkey, each relatively small in size and with no opportunity for getting together.

▶ They lived in cultures filled with pagan and occult influences.

▶ The Emperor Domitian was a dangerous man with an inferiority complex who liked to be addressed as *dominus et deus* (lord and god). Would he declare that loyalty to him was the only acceptable worship? There was obviously some persecution going on (2:13).

▶ The Jews paid a tax to the Romans so that they could follow their own religion. The Romans saw no difference between the Jews and Christians and so Christians wanted to take advantage of this loophole and maintain links with Judaism. The Jews resented this and there was a lot of tension between the two groups.

▶ Recent earthquakes, a military coup in Rome, the Jewish revolt in AD66 and the destruction of the Temple in AD70 meant they were living in turbulent times.

▶ Within the churches there was the challenge of false teaching and false prophecy. Some Christians were giving up their faith. They had thought that the Second Coming was imminent – but they were still waiting.

WORSHIP

Look at the words about Jesus that you wrote down earlier in question five. Spend some time giving thanks and worshipping Jesus for who he is and what he has done. Now take a piece of playdough. As you knead it, pray about the pressures that you and your church are under. Mould the playdough into a cross to acknowledge that Jesus will help you to withstand the pressure.

DURING THE WEEK

Set aside some time to read through the first three chapters of Revelation in one sitting. What makes the biggest impression on you? Write it down and bring it to next week's meeting. Rather than go through the churches one by one, we are going to look at themes in the letters. Next week we will look at the letters to Sardis and Laodicea.

FOR FURTHER STUDY

Study the seven letters to the churches and note down the similarities in the structure of each letter. What do you learn about Jesus, the author of the letters?

HOW ALIVE ARE YOU? – THE CHURCH AS A LIVING COMMUNITY

AIM: to consider Christ's call to a living faith today

"To the angel of the church in Sardis write:

These are the words of him who holds the seven spirits of God and the seven stars. I know your deeds; you have a reputation of being alive, but you are dead. Wake up! Strengthen what remains and is about to die, for I have not found your deeds complete in the sight of my God. Remember, therefore, what you have received and heard; obey it, and repent. But if you do not wake up, I will come like a thief, and you will not know at what time I will come to you.

Yet you have a few people in Sardis who have not soiled their clothes. They will walk with me, dressed in white, for they are worthy. He who overcomes will, like them, be dressed in white. I will never blot out his name from the book of life, but will acknowledge his name before my Father and his angels. He who has an ear, let him hear what the Spirit says to the churches."

"To the angel of the church in Laodicea write:

These are the words of the Amen, the faithful and true witness, the ruler of God's creation. I know your deeds, that you are neither cold nor hot. I wish you were either one or the other! So, because you are lukewarm—neither hot nor cold—I am about to spit you out of my mouth. You say, 'I am rich; I have acquired wealth and do not need a thing.' But you do not realize that you are wretched, pitiful, poor, blind and naked. I counsel you to buy from me gold refined in the fire, so you can become rich; and white clothes to wear, so you can cover your shameful nakedness; and salve to put on your eyes, so you can see.

Those whom I love I rebuke and discipline. So be earnest, and repent. Here I am! I stand at the door and knock. If anyone hears my voice and opens the door, I will come in and eat with him, and he with me.

To him who overcomes, I will give the right to sit with me on my throne, just as I overcame and sat down with my Father on his throne. He who has an ear, let him hear what the Spirit says to the churches."

Revelation 3:1–6, 14–22

TO SET THE SCENE

How do you know if something is alive? Think about a healthy plant – what signs of life should it show? Now think about a person – what signs of life and health do you expect to see?

Jesus was looking for signs of life in the seven churches and he didn't see many in Sardis and Laodicea. Look at the list you have made – what are the parallel signs for a healthy growing church?

Read Revelation 3:1–6 and 3:14–22

WHAT DOES SEARCH THE BIBLE SAY?

1   In the other letters we will see that Jesus begins with words of affirmation and encouragement, but not to Sardis and Laodicea. What was Jesus' verdict on them? (3:1; 3:16).

2   What were they doing wrong? Read the information boxes about the two churches to understand the relevance of what Jesus says to them.

APPLY THIS TO MY CHURCH

3   Sardis had had a good reputation, but that was in the past. Jesus is looking for signs of life now. Use the chart on page 17 to assess your church's current reputation.

HOW DOES THIS APPLY TO ME

4   Do you have a reputation – what are some of the things that you have achieved, spiritually or otherwise, in the past? Are you still learning and growing in Christ? How do you know?

HOW DOES THIS APPLY TO ME

5   Laodicea was smug and self-sufficient (3:17). How can we, in the wealthy West, remind ourselves of our dependence on God?

APPLY THIS TO
MY CHURCH

6   When was the last time that your church made a decision that required taking risks and being dependent on God?

APPLY THIS TO
MY CHURCH

7   It was the deeds of Laodicea that Jesus found insipid and useless. How do you measure whether the projects your church is involved in actually achieve anything?

8   Jesus' words are blunt, but what inspires them (3:19)?

9   What is the remedy for these churches (3:3; 3:19)? Do you need to heed these words, as a church or an individual? In what way?

Sardis and Laodicea

About Sardis

▶ Sardis was a busy trade centre that had been the capital city in the old kingdom of Lydia. Gold had been found in the river and it had been a major fashion centre, but it had suffered economic hardship.

▶ Sardis was devastated in an earthquake 80 years before Revelation was written. It had been rebuilt with Roman money, but had never quite recovered its former glory.

▶ Ancient writers used Sardis as a byword for pride coming before a fall.

About Laodicea

▶ Laodicea was a wealthy city with a thriving textile industry, famous for clothes made from black wool. It had a renowned medical school that specialised in ophthalmology.

▶ The town lacked either a hot or cold water supply. Water was pumped five miles along an aqueduct from the hot springs of Denizli. By the time it arrived it was lukewarm and poor in quality.

▶ Paul mentions this church in Colossians 4:15,16.

WORSHIP

Focus on the need to be dependent on God. Say the Lord's Prayer together – a reminder that we dependent on him for our daily bread.

Spend some time thinking about the things that make you feel secure – perhaps your job, your car, your family, your home, your relationships, your possessions. Have these become too important to you? Have you lost sight of your dependence on God? As you pray you could put symbols of these things in the centre – your wallet, car keys, house keys, mobile phone.

> *Father God, we praise you for your love for us and your generosity to us.*
> *We give to you all the things that make us feel secure and self-sufficient.*
> *We acknowledge our dependence on you.*
> *Our jobs, our homes, our relationships, our belongings have all come from you and are ours to hold lightly.*
> *We know there are so many people who don't have the things we take for granted – help us to be thankful.*
> *Help us, Lord, as we take these symbols back at the end of this evening to use them wisely.*
> *Help us never to forget our dependence on you.*
> *In the name of Jesus*
>
> ***Amen***

DURING THE WEEK

ENGAGING WITH THE WORLD Look out for people in the news – actors, sports players, politicians, celebrities – who are stuck with a past reputation. Or look for people who have managed to move on from the past and have made a fresh start. Bring one example to the group next week.

Next week we will be looking at the letter to the church in Ephesus.

FOR FURTHER STUDY

How did Jesus enable people to move on from their reputations or past experiences? Look at the woman at the well in John 4 or Zaccheus in Luke 19.

CHURCH'S REPUTATION ASSESSMENT CHART (QUESTION 3)

Fill in the name of your church and the gaps in the chart to assess the reputation it has in your area.

_____ Church

Former ministers

Known locally as the church that ...

Number in congregation at its peak

Evangelistic activities in the past ...
and the present ...

Work in the local community

Famous members of the congregation – past and present

Associated with these Christian organisations

Has sent missionaries to ...

Anything else?

In what ways does your church live up to its reputation, and in what ways does it fall short? Is that reputation a help or a hindrance?

LOVE ONE ANOTHER – THE CHURCH AS A LOVING COMMUNITY I

AIM: to explore the need to love one another as a major priority for the church

"To the angel of the church in Ephesus write:

These are the words of him who holds the seven stars in his right hand and walks among the seven golden lampstands: I know your deeds, your hard work and your perseverance. I know that you cannot tolerate wicked men, that you have tested those who claim to be apostles but are not, and have found them false. You have persevered and have endured hardships for my name, and have not grown weary.

Yet I hold this against you: You have forsaken your first love. Remember the height from which you have fallen! Repent and do the things you did at first. If you do not repent, I will come to you and remove your lampstand from its place. But you have this in your favour: You hate the practices of the Nicolaitans, which I also hate.

He who has an ear, let him hear what the Spirit says to the churches. To him who overcomes, I will give the right to eat from the tree of life, which is in the paradise of God."

Revelation 2:1–7

TO SET THE SCENE

David Beckham has his son's name tattooed on his back, his wife's name in Hindi tattooed on his arm and a guardian angel tattooed between his shoulder blades – signs of his love for his family. Talk about expressions of love – what have people done for you that have really made you feel loved?

Read Revelation 2:1–7

WHAT DOES SEARCH THE BIBLE SAY?

1   What did Jesus commend the Ephesians for? What did he hold against them?

2   The Ephesians were another church under pressure. What words of Jesus would have encouraged them that they were not forgotten and alone?

HOW DOES THIS APPLY TO ME?

3   Think back to when you first became a Christian. What did you do then that you don't do now? How do you explain the difference?

HOW DOES THIS APPLY TO ME?

4   How does meeting with other Christians – at church, in the housegroup or at other times – encourage your love for God?

APPLY THIS TO MY CHURCH

5   The Ephesians lacked love – for God and for each other. What are the hallmarks of a loving church? How much do you contribute to your church being a loving community?

6   Read the letter on Page 21. If you were Reverend Carter, how would you respond to Julie Watkins? What could the church do to help her cope with the pressure she is under?

HOW DOES THIS APPLY TO ME?

7   List the demands that are made on your time. How do you balance them all? Who controls how you spend your time?

8   Christians are commanded to love one another. Can true friendship come from a sense of duty or be organised by an institution like the church?

9   Jesus wanted the Ephesians to combine their sound teaching with love. There are lots of issues where there is the potential for Christians to disagree – divorce, the role of women and homosexuality, to name a few. How can we balance truth and love in these matters – love for both those we may disagree with and for the people involved in the issues?

'God has put into the human heart the desire to know and be known.'

Bruce Larson

Ephesus

▶ Ephesus was a bustling, thriving city – the fourth largest in the world at the time – with fabulous architecture, impressive roadways, a huge population and the most important harbour in the province.

▶ Pagan worship was everywhere. The Temple of Diana, one of the seven wonders of the world, was in Ephesus. Silversmiths made an excellent living from the worship of Diana (also known as Artemis) by making silver models of the temple (Acts 19:23–41). Ephesus was home to thousands of priests and priestesses, many of whom were sacred prostitutes.

▶ The city had a strong academic pedigree, amazing sports facilities, a huge theatre and a thriving banking system.

WORSHIP

Spend some time praying for friendships at your church. You need four paper-chain links, or strips of coloured paper and glue, plus a pen.

▶ Pray for one close friend at your church. Thank God for them and ask him to bless them.

▶ Pray for one person at the church that you'd like to get to know better, or ask God if there is someone who needs your friendship.

▶ Pray for one person that you know is in need. Is there anything you could do to help and support them?

▶ Pray for one friendship that needs healing – ask God to show you what you can do. Pray for reconciliation.

Write the name of one of these people on the paper-chain links – you don't have to tell anyone what category they come into. Glue three of the links together, and with the fourth join your small chain to a larger one until you have one long chain for the whole group.

During the week

Often we forget to tell or show people that we love and appreciate them. Make space this week to demonstrate love for one person in the church community.

Next week we will continue to look at the letter to the church at Ephesus.

FOR FURTHER STUDY

Read about the start of the church in Ephesus in Acts 18:18 to 19:41. Paul also talks about Ephesus in 1 Corinthians 16:8. Timothy spent time there as well (1 Tim. 1:3).

Letter for question 6

Dear Reverend Carter

Thank you for your sermon on Sunday about the need for the church to love each other. I wholeheartedly agree with you, but found myself nearly exploding with frustration during your talk.

I have two children and a husband who works long hours. I work part-time myself and always feel like I am spinning plates that are about to crash down around my ears, trying to balance work, housework, children, church life and time for myself.

As I sat listening to you telling me to be more loving I ran through a list of what I need to do this week: bake cakes for the school jumble sale, attend the prayer meeting for the forthcoming mission, drive my children to Cubs, football, ballet and Brownies, attend my evening class and visit my elderly mother – not to mention work and the usual shopping, cooking, cleaning and washing. 'Being more loving' towards the church just feels like one more thing on my 'to do' list. When am I supposed to find the time? Please advise me!

Yours sincerely

Julie Watkins

BEYOND THESE WALLS – THE CHURCH AS A LOVING COMMUNITY II

AIM: to consider how we can love those outside the church

"To the angel of the church in Ephesus write:

These are the words of him who holds the seven stars in his right hand and walks among the seven golden lampstands: I know your deeds, your hard work and your perseverance. I know that you cannot tolerate wicked men, that you have tested those who claim to be apostles but are not, and have found them false. You have persevered and have endured hardships for my name, and have not grown weary.

Yet I hold this against you: You have forsaken your first love. Remember the height from which you have fallen! Repent and do the things you did at first. If you do not repent, I will come to you and remove your lampstand from its place. But you have this in your favour: You hate the practices of the Nicolaitans, which I also hate.

He who has an ear, let him hear what the Spirit says to the churches. To him who overcomes, I will give the right to eat from the tree of life, which is in the paradise of God."

Revelation 2:1–7

TO SET THE SCENE
You will be asked some questions to see who knows their way around the neighbourhood. Obviously there is more to knowing a community than being a walking A to Z. Find out how many years in total people in the group have been going to the church or living in the area. What has helped you to get to know people in the community?

Read Revelation 2:1–7

WHAT DOES SEARCH THE BIBLE SAY?

1 Remind yourselves of what Jesus held against the Ephesian church. This week continues the theme of being a loving community and looks at how we can love those outside the church.

ENGAGING WITH THE WORLD

2 *'We live in the age of loneliness. In a world where marriage rates are dwindling, children are cautiously planned for..., middle age is synonymous with divorce, and old age means a nursing home, people are bound to be very lonely. Yet in spite of their aloneness, many people hunger for community.'*

Johann Christoph Arnold

Do you agree?

3 We usually associate the word love with a feeling. We talk about needing to love the lost, but how can you love people whom you haven't met and may not even get on with?

APPLY THIS TO MY CHURCH

4 The church has responded in different ways to the challenges of a lost and sometimes hostile world.

▶ Judgmental isolation: 'The world is rushing to hell and we want nothing to do with it.'

▶ Protective separation: 'The world is dangerous and we must separate ourselves from it in order to live holy lives.'

▶ Missionary engagement: 'The world is a dark place that needs the light that Christ called the church to be.'

Which of these three responses describes you – and your church? Or would you sum up your response differently?

APPLY THIS TO MY CHURCH

5 How does your church show love to the community? Think about individuals as well as organised activities.

6 If people aren't rushing to join the church, does the church need to change? Why is change so hard for us?

7 How well do you know the needs of the community around your church? How could you find out?

8 Look at the examples on Page 25 of churches that have tried new things to reach new people. Would any of these work in your area? What would be worth trying?

'The church is the only organisation that exists for the benefit of its non-members.'

Archbishop William Temple.

'I am convinced that healthy churches are changing churches. They are willing to take risks, to undertake new projects and programmes that may fail.'

Leith Anderson, A Church for the 21st Century

WORSHIP

Look at a street map of the area. Mark where group members live and go to school, college or work. Draw symbols at the edge of the map for people who live or work outside the immediate area. Mark the church and any other places where people are involved in the community. Look at the number of contacts you have with the community. Pray for these relationships, that you will be able to demonstrate the love of Christ to those outside the church.

DURING THE WEEK

Decide one thing that you can do to further a friendship with someone outside the church. It could be a phone call, an invitation to coffee, a lift to work, a drink in the pub. Ask God to bless your time together.

Next week we will be looking at the letters to the churches at Pergamum and Thyatira.

FOR FURTHER STUDY

WHAT DOES

SEARCH

THE BIBLE SAY?

Jesus says that if Ephesus does not repent he will come and remove their lampstand – in other words the church will no longer be a witness to the world. Read Mark 4:21–25 and Luke 8:16–18 to see what Jesus said about lampstands in his teaching. Israel had also been symbolised by a lampstand (Zech. 4) and had been given the calling to be a light to the Gentiles (Isa. 42:6–7), a calling that is passed on to the church.

Courageous Restructuring: examples for Question 8

In Deptford, southeast London, a group run a children's church on Saturday morning with up to 80 children. The gathering is led by children, supported by adults, with songs, games and Bible stories, aiming to do church through a child's eyes.

Alpha courses have been successfully held in the Bank of England and in the head offices of some London corporations – taking a church activity into a work environment.

At Todmorton in the Pennine foothills, a family communion service is held on Monday afternoons. Children arrive after school from 3:30pm for a drink and biscuits and the service starts at 4pm for half an hour. 'It's brought people into the worshipping life of the church who find Sunday services a bit awesome, a bit wordy and a bit middle-class,' says the vicar. Around one hundred children and adults attend each week.

A church in Wales did a survey to discover what needs existed in their locality. They have since planted a congregation in an old people's residential home with the aim of it becoming a fully-fledged church, part of the life-blood of the community, rather than a service staged by church members coming in from outside each week.

Holy Joes is a worshipping group who meet in the upper room of a pub in south London. It attracts disillusioned Christians as well as seekers who are not ready to go to church but who want a place to go where they feel comfortable, can ask questions and get honest answers.

NO COMPROMISE – THE CHURCH AS A LOYAL COMMUNITY I

 AIM: to consider what it means to be loyal to the truth

"To the angel of the church in Pergamum write:

These are the words of him who has the sharp, double-edged sword. I know where you live – where Satan has his throne. Yet you remain true to my name. You did not renounce your faith in me, even in the days of Antipas, my faithful witness, who was put to death in your city – where Satan lives.

Nevertheless, I have a few things against you: You have people there who hold to the teaching of Balaam, who taught Balak to entice the Israelites to sin by eating food sacrificed to idols and by committing sexual immorality. Likewise you also have those who hold to the teaching of the Nicolaitans. Repent therefore! Otherwise, I will soon come to you and will fight against them with the sword of my mouth.

He who has an ear, let him hear what the Spirit says to the churches. To him who overcomes, I will give some of the hidden manna. I will also give him a white stone with a new name written on it, known only to him who receives it.

"To the angel of the church in Thyatira write:

These are the words of the Son of God, whose eyes are like blazing fire and whose feet are like burnished bronze. I know your deeds, your love and faith, your service and perseverance, and that you are now doing more than you did at first.

Nevertheless, I have this against you: You tolerate that woman Jezebel, who calls herself a prophetess. By her teaching she misleads my servants into sexual immorality and the eating of food sacrificed to idols. I have given her time to repent of her immorality, but she is unwilling. So I will cast her on a bed of suffering, and I will make those who commit adultery with her suffer intensely, unless they repent of her ways. I will strike her children dead. Then all the churches will know that I am he who searches hearts and minds, and I will repay each of you according to your deeds. Now I say to the rest of you in Thyatira, to you who do not hold to her teaching and have not learned Satan's so-called deep secrets (I will not impose any other burden on you): Only hold on to what you have until I come.

To him who overcomes and does my will to the end, I will give authority over the nations—

'He will rule them with an iron sceptre;
he will dash them to pieces like pottery'—

just as I have received authority from my Father. I will also give him the morning star. He who has an ear, let him hear what the Spirit says to the churches.

Revelation 2:12–29

TO SET THE SCENE
Start with a game of Jenga. Players take it in turns to remove a block from the middle of a tower and place it on top. The one to make the tower collapse loses. Or play the flour cake game.

Read Revelation 2:12–29

1 What are Pergamum and Thyatira commended for?

2 What had these two churches done wrong?

3 The church at Pergamum had stood firm during outright opposition (v13) but is now tempted to compromise and allow false teaching to be spread. In what areas of Christian teaching does our culture tempt us to compromise?

4   Read about the trade guilds in the fact box on Thyatira. We face the same question on different issues: should we do what everyone else does or make a stand as Christians? What are the arguments for behaving like everyone else?

What are the arguments for making a stand and being different? How do you decide which to do – where do you draw the line?

5   Jesus wanted these two churches to be loyal to the truth. But what is the truth – what do you consider to be the non-negotiables of the Christian faith?

6   Christians disagree about some areas of behaviour – for example, some are teetotal because of their faith; others enjoy alcohol in moderation.

What influences these different understandings of how a Christian should behave?

HOW DOES THIS

APPLY TO ME

7   Sexual immorality was a big temptation for the two churches – nothing much has changed. What will help us to resist sexual immorality?

8   Jesus has called several of the churches to repent and Pergamum and Thyatira are no exception. What does it mean to repent?

WORSHIP

This evening, you will be given some space for reflection. Are there times where you have compromised your faith? Have you been tempted to be disloyal to the truth? Have you kept yourself pure? Ask the Holy Spirit to show you if you need to repent.

Pour yourself some iced water and drink it to symbolise God's cleansing of you from within. Read Psalm 51 and thank God for his forgiveness.

DURING THE WEEK

Repentance is not done easily or lightly. Follow up in the week anything you felt the Holy Spirit bring to your mind. Continue to pray. Talk and pray with a trusted friend. Is there anything you need to do to put things right?

Next week we will continue to look at the letters to Pergamum and Thyatira.

FOR FURTHER STUDY

WHAT DOES Look at what Jesus said about the truth in John's gospel. John 1:14–17;
SEARCH 8:31–32; 14:6,7,15–17; 16:12–15; 18:37. Count up how many times Jesus
says 'I tell you the truth...' in John's gospel. (A concordance makes this
THE BIBLE SAY? a lot easier.)

> 'We must preserve unity in essentials, liberty in non-essentials and charity in all things.'
>
> **Rupert Meldenius**

Pergamum and Thyatira

About Pergamum

▶ Pergamum had the feel of an old academic city, like Oxford or Cambridge. It had a fabulous library that held over 200,000 hand-written books. The Romans had made the city the capital of Asia.

▶ Jesus used strong language about the city, calling it the throne of Satan. This is probably because of the strong historical commitment to emperor worship.

▶ There were also lots of opportunities to worship different idols. There was a prominent altar to Zeus on the skyline of the city with smoke rising all day from the sacrifices. It was impossible to miss it.

About Thyatira

▶ Thyatira was a busy, wealthy market city, a centre for the wool trade and the dyeing industry. Lydia, the seller of purple in Acts 16:14, came from here.

▶ Anyone who wanted to do business in the city had to be a member of a trade guild. This caused a dilemma for the Christians. If they didn't join, they couldn't make a living. If they joined, they were expected to attend banquets and eat meat that had been sacrificed to idols.

HOLD ON – THE CHURCH AS A LOYAL COMMUNITY II

AIM: to learn about the need for discipline and the fruits of faithfulness

"To the angel of the church in Pergamum write:

These are the words of him who has the sharp, double-edged sword. I know where you live – where Satan has his throne. Yet you remain true to my name. You did not renounce your faith in me, even in the days of Antipas, my faithful witness, who was put to death in your city – where Satan lives.

Nevertheless, I have a few things against you: You have people there who hold to the teaching of Balaam, who taught Balak to entice the Israelites to sin by eating food sacrificed to idols and by committing sexual immorality. Likewise you also have those who hold to the teaching of the Nicolaitans. Repent therefore! Otherwise, I will soon come to you and will fight against them with the sword of my mouth.

He who has an ear, let him hear what the Spirit says to the churches. To him who overcomes, I will give some of the hidden manna. I will also give him a white stone with a new name written on it, known only to him who receives it.

"To the angel of the church in Thyatira write:

These are the words of the Son of God, whose eyes are like blazing fire and whose feet are like burnished bronze. I know your deeds, your love and faith, your service and perseverance, and that you are now doing more than you did at first.

Nevertheless, I have this against you: You tolerate that woman Jezebel, who calls herself a prophetess. By her teaching she misleads my servants into sexual immorality and the eating of food sacrificed to idols. I have given her time to repent of her immorality, but she is unwilling. So I will cast her on a bed of suffering, and I will make those who commit adultery with her suffer intensely, unless they repent of her ways. I will strike her children dead. Then all the churches will know that I am he who searches hearts and minds, and I will repay each of you according to your deeds. Now I say to the rest of you in Thyatira, to you who do not hold to her teaching and have not learned Satan's so-called deep secrets (I will not impose any other burden on you): Only hold on to what you have until I come.

To him who overcomes and does my will to the end, I will give authority over the nations—

'He will rule them with an iron sceptre;
he will dash them to pieces like pottery'—

just as I have received authority from my Father. I will also give him the morning star. He who has an ear, let him hear what the Spirit says to the churches.

Revelation 2:12–29

TO SET THE SCENE

Find out who has worked for a long time to achieve something; perhaps training for a marathon; or studying for a qualification while working; or creating a tapestry or knitting a jumper. Was anyone tempted to give up? What kept you going? Was it worth it?

Read Revelation 2:12–29

WHAT DOES SEARCH THE BIBLE SAY?

1   Remind yourself of the situation in Thyatira. What did Jesus commend them for? What were they doing wrong?

APPLY THIS TO MY CHURCH

2   Jezebel had a strong influence in the church and was abusing two gifts – prophecy and leadership. What implications might this have had in the future for people exercising the gift of prophecy, or women who felt called to

leadership? What is your church's attitude to prophecy and women in leadership?

WHAT DOES **SEARCH** THE BIBLE SAY?

3   The Thyatirans were guilty of tolerating false teaching, rather like the Corinthian church. In his letters to the Corinthians Paul highlights two extremes that we can fall into when faced with sin in the church. What are they (1 Cor. 5:1–5; 2 Cor. 2:5–11)?

HOW DOES THIS APPLY TO ME

Which do you tend towards?

4   Paul challenged the Corinthians to discipline those in the church who were sinning. What should be the motivation of church discipline? And what should be its goal?

5   Two people in a church are separately involved in the same immoral situation, say claiming benefits while working. One is a new Christian and the other has been a Christian for years. Should the church treat them differently?

WHAT DOES **SEARCH** THE BIBLE SAY?

6 Jesus shows how truth can triumph over falsehood by reminding the church that he has a sharp double-edged sword. Look at Revelation 1:16 and Hebrews 4:12–13 – what does this sword symbolise?

7   Jesus tells the church to hold on to the end and remain faithful. What is promised to those who overcome in these two churches? What about in the other churches?

8   What other words of encouragement would the churches have found in these letters?

HOW DOES THIS APPLY TO ME

9   How would you encourage someone who was having a hard time and was tempted to give up on their faith?

WORSHIP

Share communion together as a housegroup as a reminder of Christ's victory over sin. Jesus invites us to share this meal with him regularly, a forerunner to the banquet we will share with him in his new kingdom. Invite group members to take away a white stone with them, to remind them of forgiveness, acceptance and a future life with Christ.

DURING THE WEEK

ENGAGING WITH Look out for stories in the news of people who have persevered – perhaps athletes who have a strict training regime, or an author who has been persistent in seeking publication, or someone who has pursued justice. THE WORLD What can you learn from them?

Next week we will be looking at the letters to the churches at Smyrna and Philadelphia.

FOR FURTHER STUDY

WHAT DOES Read up on prophecy in the early church. For example, read Acts 13:1–12; 21:10–15; 27:21–44. What guidance does Paul give for the use of prophecy? (1 Cor. 14:1–5, 26–33). Some churches almost ignore this gift, THE BIBLE SAY? while others seem to go a bit overboard – what does your church do?

FAITHFUL UNDER PRESSURE – THE CHURCH AS A LONG SUFFERING COMMUNITY

AIM: to consider suffering as a normal part of the Christian life

"To the angel of the church in Smyrna write:

These are the words of him who is the First and the Last, who died and came to life again. I know your afflictions and your poverty – yet you are rich! I know the slander of those who say they are Jews and are not, but are a synagogue of Satan. Do not be afraid of what you are about to suffer. I tell you, the devil will put some of you in prison to test you, and you will suffer persecution for ten days. Be faithful, even to the point of death, and I will give you the crown of life.

He who has an ear, let him hear what the Spirit says to the churches. He who overcomes will not be hurt at all by the second death."

"To the angel of the church in Philadelphia write:

These are the words of him who is holy and true, who holds the key of David. What he opens no one can shut, and what he shuts no one can open. I know your deeds. See, I have placed before you an open door that no one can shut. I know that you have little strength, yet you have kept my word and have not denied my name. I will make those who are of the synagogue of Satan, who claim to be Jews though they are not, but are liars—I will make them come and fall down at your feet and acknowledge that I have loved you. Since you have kept my command to endure patiently, I will also keep you from the hour of trial that is going to come upon the whole world to test those who live on the earth.

I am coming soon. Hold on to what you have, so that no one will take your crown. Him who overcomes I will make a pillar in the temple of my God. Never again will he leave it. I will write on him the name of my God and the name of the city of my God, the new Jerusalem, which is coming down out of heaven from my God; and I will also write on him my new name. He who has an ear, let him hear what the Spirit says to the churches.

Revelation 2:8–11, 3:7–13

TO SET THE SCENE

Use the chart on Page 39, to think back over the joys and hard times of your life. Mark the intervals on the time axis to represent five or ten years, depending on your age. Draw a line to show the ups and downs of your life and add words to help remind yourself of what was happening. You may have had times of both blessing and suffering or hardship at the same time – feel free to make the chart your own.

How do you feel now about the difficult times? Has good ever come out of them? Were you aware that God was close to you in those times?

Read Revelation 2:8–11, 3:7–13

WHAT DOES
SEARCH
THE BIBLE SAY?

1 What is different about Jesus' words to these two churches compared with the other letters?

HOW DOES THIS
APPLY TO ME

2 Have you ever thought that Jesus might commend you for something? Why do some of us feel that God can never really be pleased or satisfied with us?

These two letters were written to churches facing strong opposition who knew the reality of suffering. The problem of pain and suffering is very complex and can't be covered in one week's study, but some helpful principles can be found in these texts.

APPLY THIS TO
MY CHURCH
3   Suffering is part of the normal Christian life. Often the way we communicate the gospel portrays Christians as happy, successful and secure. Should we include the reality of suffering in our evangelism? How?

4   How many Christians do you think died for their faith in 1999? How can we respond to this fact?

HOW DOES THIS
APPLY TO ME
5   Suffering must be faced with an eternal perspective. What future promises does Jesus give the believers in Smyrna and Philadelphia? Christians usually try to ensure that they are not 'so heavenly minded that they are no earthly use', but is there a danger that we don't think enough about eternal life?

6   Suffering does not mean desertion. What words in these letters would encourage the Christians that they are not alone? How have you reminded yourself of God's presence when he seems far away?

APPLY THIS TO
MY CHURCH
7   Success is measured differently by Jesus. The Sermon on the Mount shows that Jesus came to establish an upside-down kingdom, where the poor in spirit and the persecuted are blessed. How is this reflected in his encouragement to Smyrna (2:9) and Philadelphia (3:8)? Is your church faithful, or successful? Or both?

HOW DOES THIS
APPLY TO ME
8   Suffering and opportunity often coexist together. Philadelphia were told that they had 'an open door that no one can shut' even though they were weak. Is this true in your experience? Have you ever been through a difficult time that has led to positive new things?

ENGAGING WITH
THE WORLD
9   Which of these principles do you think contrasts most strongly with our culture's attitudes to suffering?

WORSHIP

Put a lit candle in the centre of the room. If you can, put some thorns around it to remind you of Christ's suffering.

Read Psalm 13

Pray for the persecuted church – that they would have the courage to endure; that the hearts of their oppressors would be touched by the love of Christ; that you will remember to keep praying for them. Light a small candle for each person that you pray for. Pray for any other people known to you who are suffering.

DURING THE WEEK

 ENGAGING WITH Ask God to show you how you can be a means of encouragement and support to someone who is suffering. When you read the newspaper or watch the news, spend a few minutes praying for anyone who is suffering, THE WORLD that it will be an opportunity for God to minister his love to them.

Next week come prepared to talk about what you have learned from this study of Revelation.

FOR FURTHER STUDY

Get some information on the persecuted church around the world by contacting Release International (www.every3minutes.com) or Voice of the Martyrs (www.persecution.com). Group members may have organisations they already support that you could contact.

> *'I have served him for eighty-six years, and he has done me no wrong; how then can I blaspheme the king who saved me?'*
>
> ***Polycarp, leader of the church at Smyrna, replying***
> ***when commanded to renounce Christ***

Smyrna and Philadelphia

About Smyrna

▶ Smyrna was a beautiful city known as 'the glory of Asia'. It was a deep-water port, with wide, well-planned streets and a huge theatre. It enjoyed a flourishing trade in wines and was also famous for its science and medicine.

▶ The city had been destroyed by an earthquake in 600BC and had been rebuilt from nothing.

▶ The city was spread extensively over the summit of Mount Pagus, giving it the appearance of a crown when viewed from a distance.

About Philadelphia

▶ Philadelphia was built close to a live volcano. This brought benefits in terms of rich soil which was ideal for growing vines, and hot springs where the sick came to bathe in soothing waters.

▶ However, the volcano also meant danger – new cracks were said to appear in the walls of buildings every day. The city had been destroyed in AD17 and rebuilt. Because of the volcano the citizens were very unsettled, fleeing for their lives whenever the tremors came.

▶ It was a very pagan city; the principle god was Dionysius, the god of wine.

LIFE CHART FOR SET THE SCENE

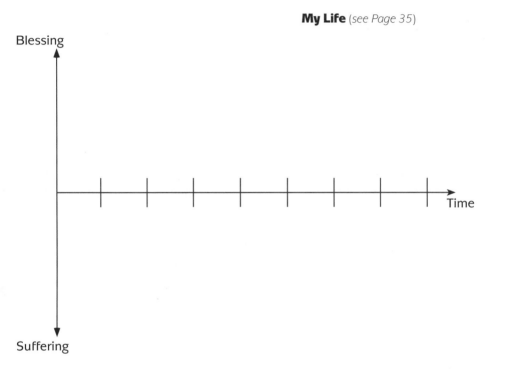

My Life (*see Page 35*)

Blessing

Time

Suffering

AN OPEN DOOR – THE CHURCH AS A WITNESSING COMMUNITY

 AIM: to consider the open doors that might be in front of us

"To the angel of the church in Philadelphia write:

"These are the words of him who is holy and true, who holds the key of David. What he opens no one can shut, and what he shuts no one can open. I know your deeds. See, I have placed before you an open door that no one can shut. I know that you have little strength, yet you have kept my word and have not denied my name. I will make those who are of the synagogue of Satan, who claim to be Jews though they are not, but are liars – I will make them come and fall down at your feet and acknowledge that I have loved you. Since you have kept my command to endure patiently, I will also keep you from the hour of trial that is going to come upon the whole world to test those who live on the earth.

"I am coming soon. Hold on to what you have, so that no one will take your crown. Him who overcomes I will make a pillar in the temple of my God. Never again will he leave it. I will write on him the name of my God and the name of the city of my God, the new Jerusalem, which is coming down out of heaven from my God; and I will also write on him my new name. He who has an ear, let him hear what the Spirit says to the churches."

Revelation 3:7–13

TO SET THE SCENE:

How did you become a Christian? Can you pinpoint the moment of conversion, or was it more of a process? Who or what was instrumental in your decision to follow Christ?

Read Revelation 3:7–13

1   Discuss how you feel about evangelism – sharing the gospel with those who don't know Jesus. Where would your feelings on evangelism be on a scale of one to ten, where one is the prospect of having a filling at the dentist without anaesthetic, and ten is how you feel on the night before a world cruise on a luxury yacht?

2   Jesus says that he sets an open door in front of the Philadelphians that no one can shut. This is seen as an encouragement that the time is ripe for them to proclaim the gospel; the city built as a mission outpost for Greek culture can become a mission centre for Christ (see box on Page 43). Look at the times that Paul uses a similar phrase: 1 Corinthians 16:8–9; Colossians 4:3; 2 Corinthians 2:12.

3   What excuses might the Philadelphians have made for not being able to seize this opportunity?

4   What areas of possible opportunity are there for you to communicate the gospel, through words or actions? Write down the areas of life you are involved in, where you meet and interact with people.

5   What excuses might we make or reasons might we give for not talking about or demonstrating the gospel in these areas?

6 Jesus is very clear in this letter that he has opened the door of opportunity – it is not something that the Philadelphians can do for themselves.(v7, 8). How can we recognise when Jesus has opened a door for us? Look again at the areas you wrote down in question 4 – where might the open doors be here?

7 If Jesus has opened doors for us, what can we do about the excuses or reasons we thought up for not getting involved?

8 Look back at how group members came Christians – does this give you some ideas for where you might start?

WORSHIP
What have you learned from this study of Revelation? Give everyone a chance to share one thing. Pray, thanking God for the opportunity to study his word and pray that the group will be able to act on it in the future.

Look at the areas of opportunity open to the group. Spend some time praying, that you will be able to discern the open doors that Jesus has set before you and that you will be willing to respond.

More about Philadelphia
The city of Philadelphia was originally built as a mission outpost for Greek civilisation and culture. It sat on the borders of Mysia, Lydia and Phrygia and was the last bastion of Greek thinking before the wilderness of the barbarians began. The city was built with the objective of converting the barbarians of Phrygia to the Greek way of thinking – a mission that had been most unsuccessful.

DURING THE WEEK
Continue to pray about the open doors that Jesus has set before you, both as an individual and as part of the church – that it will be clear what they are and that you will be able to make the most of them. It may be helpful to meet up with a couple of friends to encourage each other, or to make sure that you keep talking and praying about it in the housegroup.

FOR FURTHER STUDY
In I Corinthians Paul says that a great door for effective work has opened for him in Ephesus and there are many who oppose him. This was also the experience of the early church in Acts – opportunities for evangelism provoked opposition. Read through Acts to find out more about how the church dealt with this. For example: who was opposed to their message? Acts 4:1–4; 6:8–15; 12:1–5; 13:4–12. What significant event brought a period of peace? Acts 9, particularly v31. What was their reaction to opposition? Acts 13:45–52; 16:25. What can you learn from their experience?

LEADERS' GUIDE

TO HELP YOU LEAD

You may have led a housegroup many times before or this may be your first time. Here is some advice on how to lead these studies:

▶ As a group leader, you don't have to be an expert or a lecturer. You are there to facilitate the learning of the group members – helping them to discover for themselves the wisdom in God's word. You should not be doing most of the talking or dishing out the answers, whatever the group expects from you!

▶ You do need to be aware of the group's dynamics, however. People can be quite quick to label themselves and each other in a group situation. One person might be seen as the expert, another the moaner who always has something to complain about. One person may be labelled as quiet and not be expected to contribute; another person may always jump in with something to say. Be aware of the different type of individuals in the group, but don't allow the labels to stick. You may need to encourage those who find it hard to get a word in, and quieten down those who always have something to say. Talk to members between sessions to find out how they feel about the group.

▶ The sessions are planned to try and engage every member in actively learning. Of course you cannot force anyone to take part if they don't want to, but it won't be too easy to be a spectator. Activities that ask everyone to write down a word, or to talk in twos and then report back to the group, are there for a reason. They give everyone space to think and form their opinion, even if not everyone voices it out loud.

▶ Do adapt the sessions for your group as you feel is appropriate. Some groups may know each other very well and will be prepared to talk at a deep level. New groups may take a bit of time to get to know each other before making themselves vulnerable, but encourage members to share their lives with each other.

▶ Encourage a number of replies to each question. The study is not about finding a single right answer, but about sharing experiences and thoughts in order to find out how to apply the Bible to people's lives. When brainstorming, don't be too quick to evaluate the contributions. Write everything down and then have a look to see which suggestions are worth keeping.

▶ Similarly encourage everyone to ask questions, to voice doubts and to discuss difficulties. Some parts of the Bible are difficult to understand. Sometimes the Christian faith throws up paradoxes. Painful things happen to us that make it difficult to see what God is doing. A housegroup should be a safe place to express all of this. If discussion doesn't resolve the issue, send everyone away to pray about it, in between sessions, and ask your minister for advice!

▶ Give yourself time in the week to read through the Bible passage and the questions. Read the Leaders' notes for the session, as different ways of presenting the questions are sometimes suggested. However, during the session, don't be too quick to come in with the answer – sometimes we need space to think.

▶ Delegate as much as you like! The easiest activities to delegate are reading the text, and the worship suggestions, but there are other ways to involve group members. Giving people responsibility can help them own the session much more.

▶ Pray for group members by name, that God would meet with them during the week. Pray for the group session, for a constructive and helpful time. Ask the Lord to equip you as you lead the group.

THE STRUCTURE OF EACH SESSION

Feedback: find out what people remember from the previous session, or if they have been able to act during the week on what was discussed last time.

To set the scene: an activity or a question to get everyone thinking about the subject to be studied.

Bible reading: it's important actually to read the passage you are studying during the session. Ask someone to prepare this in advance or go round the group reading a verse or two each. Don't assume everyone will be happy to read out loud.

Questions and activities: adapt these as appropriate to your group. Some groups may enjoy a more activity-based approach, some may prefer just to discuss the questions. Try out some new things!

Worship: suggestions for creative worship and prayer are included, which give everyone an opportunity to respond to God, largely individually. Use these alongside singing or other group expressions of worship. Add in a prayer time with opportunities to pray for group members and their families and friends.

During the week: this gives a specific task to do during the week, helping people to continue to think about or apply what they have learned.

For further study: Suggestions are given for those people who want to study the themes further. These could be included in the housegroup if you feel it is appropriate and if there is time.

WHAT YOU NEED

A list of materials that are needed is printed at the start of each session in the Leaders' guide. In addition you will probably need:

Bibles: the Bible passage is printed in the book so that all the members can work from the same version. It will be useful to have other Bibles available, or to ask everyone to bring their own, so that other passages can be referred to.

Paper and pens: for people who need more space than is in the book!

Flip chart: it is helpful to write down people's comments during a brainstorming session, so that none of the suggestions is lost. There may not be space for a proper flip chart in the average lounge, and having one may make it feel too much like a business meeting or lecture. Try getting someone to write on a big sheet of paper on the floor or coffee table, and then stick this up on the wall with blu-tack.

GROUND RULES

How do people know what is expected of them in a housegroup situation? Is it ever discussed, or do we just pick up cues from each other? You may find it helpful to discuss some ground rules for the housegroup at the start of this course, even if your group has been going a long time. This also gives you an opportunity to talk about how you, as the leader, see the group. Ask everyone to think about what they want to get out of the course. How do they want the group to work? What values do they want to be part of the group's experience; honesty, respect, confidentiality? How do they want their contributions to be treated? You could ask everyone to write down three ground rules on slips of paper and put them in a bowl. Pass the bowl round the group. Each person takes out a rule and reads it, and someone collates a list. Discuss the ground rules that have been suggested and come up with a top five. This method enables everyone to contribute fairly anonymously. Alternatively, if your group are all quite vocal, have a straight discussion about it!

NB not all questions in each session are covered, some are self-explanatory

ICONS

AIM

The aim of the session

ENGAGING WITH THE WORLD

Engaging with the world

WHAT DOES THE BIBLE SAY?

Investigate what else the Bible says

HOW DOES THIS APPLY TO ME

How does this apply to me?

APPLY THIS TO MY CHURCH

What about our church?

www.springharvest.org/workbooks/

SESSION 1

MATERIALS NEEDED

▶ Crossword puzzles – cryptic and straightforward
▶ A large sheet of paper and pens
▶ Playdough or plasticine

TO SET THE SCENE

Have a few newspaper crosswords available, for people to do as they have coffee at the start of the housegroup. Introduce the book that you will be studying. Revelation is one of the most misunderstood books of the Bible. People either ignore it, or get obsessed with it. Some people treat it like a cryptic crossword puzzle, straining to find the hidden meanings or decipher the symbols. In fact, it is a call to genuine discipleship in the face of great pressure. It is a book that gives a fresh vision of Jesus, especially in these first three chapters.

1 Some people might see Revelation as a horror film – full of images of what will happen to sinners. Others might see it as a foreign language film – completely incomprehensible. In terms of mail, some might see it as a tax return form – you know you need to deal with it one day, but you put it off as long as possible. Some might see it as a love letter – from God. Ask who has actually read all of Revelation, how often and how recently. This is not to make people feel guilty if they haven't but to find out if their feelings are based on experience or the book's reputation.

2 Revelation is about Jesus Christ and his power and might. It promises blessing to those who take note of it.

3 Some possible similarities: we have many pagan and materialistic influences in our culture which threaten to shape our thinking and behaviour. We too are waiting for Jesus and longing for our churches to be fruitful. There are disagreements between different denominations as well as misunderstandings between religions. At the time of writing we are seeing very turbulent times, acts of terrorism, war and people in need.

4 You could give people a few moments to write these down in their workbooks, and then discuss them with others if they want to.

5 Verses 12–16 give a description of how John saw Jesus. As a group, build up a

word image. On a large piece of paper, write 'Jesus' in the centre and around it write down the facts that you find in the verses. There are things to pick out in verses 5, 6, 7, 8, 13, 16, 17 and 18 (and probably more!) Use this piece of paper as a focus during the worship.

6   Some of the events in Revelation have happened – the churches have all had their chance to respond to the words of Jesus. The early church understood the second coming to be imminent – if it was near for them, it must be much nearer for us. These words should remind us that we need to be ready for Jesus to come again.

7   It is very easy to be critical about the church, and to stand outside it talking about 'them', forgetting that we are part of it. A code of conduct could include a desire for honesty, talking about 'we' not 'they', including constructive comments for how group members can make a difference, not blaming individuals. The group will need to decide what is most appropriate for them, and could make a record of the code in their workbooks. The code will be useful when you see the 'what about our church?' icon.

WORSHIP
Put the paper you wrote on in question five in the centre of the group to act as a focus. Encourage people to start with expressing thanks and worship to Jesus for who he is and what he has done. Supply some playdough or plasticine that people can squeeze and knead as they consider and pray about the pressures they are under.

FOR FURTHER STUDY
The letters follow this pattern:

◗   The name of the church that the letter is written to
◗   Who the letter is from – 'these are the words of him who...'
◗   What Jesus knows about the church
◗   His assessment of their condition – you are rich (2:9), you are dead (3:1)
◗   His command to them
◗   He who has an ear, let him hear...
◗   A promise for those who overcome

SESSION 2

MATERIALS NEEDED
- You could have a plant as a visual aid for 'to set the scene' – either healthy or half-dead!
- A cross or Bible for the worship

FEEDBACK
Over coffee at the start, find out what impression the first three chapters of Revelation made on group members.

TO SET THE SCENE
A plant will have strong, green leaves, not floppy ones. It will be growing new leaves and/or bearing fruit. Some plants turn towards the light.

People breathe; eat, drink and grow; relate to others; start very dependent, learn some independence, need to be interdependent; learn new things; express themselves.

1 Sardis is described as dead. Laodicea makes Jesus feel sick – he wants to spit them out of his mouth – and they are sleepy and smug. Neither shows signs of healthy life.

2 Sardis leaves projects unfinished (3:2) and is morally compromised – the soiled clothes referred to in 3:4. They need to wake up and be watchful (3:2). Laodicea is ineffective (3:15) and smug and self-sufficient (3:17). They are deceiving themselves, unaware that they are really poor and blind (3:17).

3 You may want to remind people of the code written last week! Encourage people to think about how the church is now compared to how it has been. Reputation can be a dangerous thing, encouraging us to see ourselves as others see us and live in the past. A bad reputation can also be a hindrance – people can be reluctant to acknowledge change. Or we may be in love with what happened in the past and refuse to move on.

4 As individuals we need to be continually growing in Christ, not just living on our past experiences. That doesn't mean we always feel very close to God or have one amazing spiritual experience after another. Thinking back to the plant analogy at the start: during the winter plants often look dead, but in the spring they show signs of fresh life. Think about the parallels in our spiritual lives.

5   It is very easy for us to take for granted that our standard of living will continue to rise. Most of us tend to spend just a bit more than we earn and think life would be easier if we had a little bit more money. To remind ourselves of our dependence on God, we can look at the way most people in the world live, hear stories of Christians who live by faith or have chosen to live amongst poor people, and put ourselves in the place where we need to be dependent.

6   You could also invite people to respond to this question personally.

7   A difficult question! Setting targets for work of a spiritual nature seems wrong – how can we dictate what God will do? But it is important to know what need we are trying to meet, or what goal we are aiming for. Setting up a system of monitoring and evaluation is important so that we can see if we are using money wisely.

8   This discipline comes from a heart of love. Ask parents in the group to talk about how it feels to discipline children. See also Hebrews 12:4–13.

9   Repentance, sincerity and obedience. You may like to give people an opportunity to think about this on their own.

WORSHIP

Set a cross or a Bible in the centre of the room, as a symbol of God's love. Explain to people what will happen during the worship time, so they can be ready to put their wallets etc by the cross or Bible if they want to. You could play some background music while people reflect to help them relax. The prayer could be said together, or one person could read it on behalf of the whole group.

SESSION 3

MATERIALS NEEDED
Gummed paper-chain links, or strips of coloured paper and glue, plus pens

FEEDBACK
Ask people to talk about the examples they found of people who are hampered by a bad reputation, or who have made a fresh start. Is there anything to learn from them?

TO SET THE SCENE

You could bring an up-to-date example of a celebrity declaring their love extravagantly – is this a meaningful symbol of love? Ask for examples from people's lives – not just romantic love, but friendship and family love as well.

1   The Ephesians were commended for their deeds, their hard work, and their perseverance. They did not tolerate wicked men, had tested and found out false apostles and hated the practices of the Nicolaitans. (Not much is known about these people.) Jesus holds against them the fact that they have forsaken their first love – this refers to love of God as well as love for each other.

2   Jesus is holding onto the church, and walks among them (v1). He knows them, being aware of their struggles and what they are doing. He promises the right to eat from the tree of life to those who overcome.

3   This is not intended to make people feel guilty! Some of the change can be down to now being in a different phase of life. Those who have family and work responsibilities don't have as much free time as they might have done when they first became Christians. Should we expect to maintain the joy and enthusiasm we may have felt when we first met Jesus?

4   Allow honesty – perhaps it doesn't! Some people have left the church in frustration and are still Christians, but we are told not to give up the habit of meeting together (Heb. 10:25). Encourage people to focus on the positives.

5   We know that we're all meant to love each other and that can create a superficial veneer of 'Christianised friendships' rather than really loving relationships. How do people who love each other treat each other? Make a list as you brainstorm. Some things that may come up: fellowship – spending time together; praying for one another; honesty and reality; encouraging one another; bearing one another's burdens; sorting out conflicts; hospitality; sharing resources; forgiveness and reconciliation; serving one another.

You may want to encourage quiet reflection for the second question.

6   This letter may strike a chord with others who feel the same way, so be sensitive to the fact that some people will be talking about themselves in the guise of talking about Julie.

8   Not an easy question to answer! The important thing is that people are able to make close friendships – these don't have to be at church. You could ask people what changes might help them to invest more in friendships at church.

9   Don't let this get side-tracked into a discussion of the issues – get people to talk about how to keep truth and love in balance. In reality there will always be a tension between the two. We need to be honest with ourselves about whether we naturally emphasise one over the other, and try to redress the balance.

WORSHIP
Lead people through the time of prayer, by introducing each category and perhaps praying a general prayer at the end of a few minutes before moving on to the next category.

The paper-chain could be hung up in future weeks when the housegroup meet to remind them of the friendships they have prayed for.

SESSION 4

MATERIALS NEEDED
▶   A map of the local area (see worship instructions below)
▶   Coloured pens

FEEDBACK
It probably won't be appropriate to get specific feedback on how people showed love to others in the church community – but you could ask general questions about how it went.

TO SET THE SCENE
Devise a quiz. Give a starting point, and then a series of directions and ask where people will end up. For example, 'start with your back to W H Smiths on the High Street. Turn left, take the first right, second left and walk about one hundred yards down the road. Where are you?' You only need about four or five questions.

Members of some housegroups may come from far and wide and may not all belong to the same geographical community, so adjust the material in this session accordingly. You can ask people to answer the questions for the community where they live or work.

1   They had forsaken their first love.

3   Love is also a decision and an action. Ask if anyone has found that they have grown to love someone <u>after</u> they did something for them, rather than before.

4   Denominations have had different emphases in the past – sometimes these can linger in our attitudes even if we have mentally moved on.

6   Some people are experimenting with different forms of church while others emphasise the need to teach the basics to help people cope with what has always happened. Change involves risk and can be uncomfortable. It can challenge our perceptions of ourselves.

7   Ask people to think about which community they feel most part of, if not everyone shares a common geographical community. Some churches have done surveys of the area, or found out statistics from the local library.

WORSHIP
Use a street map of the area around the church if that is where people come from. Otherwise draw a rough map of a larger area that will include everyone. People can use different coloured pens to mark where they live and so on.

SESSION 5

MATERIALS NEEDED
▶   Jenga game or ingredients for the flour cake game
▶   A jug of iced water and a glass for each person
▶   A bottle of olive oil and one of red wine vinegar

FEEDBACK
Again, specific feedback on the task for last week is probably not appropriate. You could ask how people are finding the study of Revelation. Would they revise their comparisons to films and items of post that were made is Session One?

TO SET THE SCENE
If you haven't got the game Jenga, ask around – someone in the housegroup is likely to have it. If you can't get hold of one, play the flour cake game instead. Pack a small mixing bowl to the brim with flour and turn it out onto a plate. Add a sweet

to the top. Players take it in turns to cut a slice from the cake and push it to one side without making the sweet fall. The person who topples the sweet has to pick it up from the flour with their teeth.

This week you will be studying the need to hold onto truth. Removing elements of truth from our faith can cause it to become unstable and collapse like a Jenga tower.

1   Pergamum – staying true to Christ's name even in times of outright opposition. Thyatira – deeds, love, faith, service and perseverance and doing more than they did at first.

2   Pergamum – allowing false teaching to affect the behaviour of some in the church. Thyatira – giving space to a false prophet. In both churches some people were eating meat sacrificed to idols and indulging in sexual immorality.

3   You might include: sexuality – sex before marriage, cohabitation, attitudes towards homosexuality; occult and new age influences – some children's TV programmes making these more acceptable; consumerism rather than trusting God to provide.

4   Arguments for behaving like everyone else: we are called to 'salt' society – how can we do that from a distance? How can we relate Christ to the culture if we are not involved in the culture? How can we befriend those outside the church if we are not involved with them? Arguments for being different: how will people know we are Christians if we are not distinctive? We are called to be holy and need to be separate.

5   This debate could take all night! John Stott says that there are two non-negotiables: the truth about Christ – that he is the Son of God, that he died and rose again, that he saves the world from sin – and the truth about holiness – that genuine belief will affect behaviour, although there is room for opinions on exactly how.

6   The history and tradition of the denomination they are in; what is acceptable in the culture around them; their understanding of Scripture; the leadership style in their church – some are more prescriptive than others.

7   Talking about it – Christians don't seem to find it easy to discuss sexuality; being accountable to a close friend; avoiding areas of temptation such as books, films and Internet sites; being open and honest; not responding as if sexual sin was worse than any other.

8   Repentance means to return to dependence on God. It indicates a complete change in attitude towards sin and God, a turning away from sin to righteousness and being made right with God again. It goes beyond being sorry to changed behaviour.

WORSHIP
As a visual aid, have a bottle containing about equal parts of olive oil and red wine vinegar. Shake the bottle. This is representative of the compromise we sometimes get drawn into as Christians, where everything is muddled together. Allow the mixture to stand and watch the oil and vinegar separate. We can pray that God makes it clear to us how to behave so we are not mixed up in wrong things. Have a jug of iced water and a glass each so everyone can drink to symbolise God's cleansing.

Read Psalm 51 – David's prayer for forgiveness. Remind people of God's forgiveness, either using some words from your church's liturgy or by reading 1 John 1:5–9.

SESSION 6

MATERIALS NEEDED
- Bread and wine to celebrate communion together, with some liturgy if appropriate
- A white stone for each member – you can get these at a garden centre
- A large sheet of paper and marker pen

TO SET THE SCENE
You could ask someone who has spent a long time on a craft such as tapestry, pottery, carpentry, photography or knitting to bring in their handiwork for everyone to see.

1   Thyatira was commended for their deeds, love, faith, service and perseverance and doing more than they did at first. Their sin was that they had given space

to a false prophet, resulting in some people thinking it was fine to eat meat sacrificed to idols and to indulge in sexual immorality. Paul writes about meat sacrificed to idols in 1 Corinthians 8–10 and Romans 14. Most meat available in the markets would have been surplus from the pagan temples. Paul believed Christians could eat this meat because association with idols that represented gods that didn't exist would not contaminate it. However, if eating the meat caused problems for others, or made people think that the Christians were involved in idol worship, then they should, he said, abstain. The feasts in the guilds, however, were essentially religious occasions that took place in the temple, so any Christian eating meat there was taking part in a religious activity that would compromise their faith. 'Jezebel' was probably a nickname to expose her true character – she was similar to Queen Jezebel who had worshipped Baal with King Ahab and had spread her teaching of idolatry throughout Israel (I Kgs. 16:31–33 and 2 Kgs. 9:22).

2   The danger is that having had a bad experience of false prophecy or a bad response to prophecy, we then become overly suspicious of all prophecy or end up rejecting it altogether without examining the biblical teaching. The same can be true for women in leadership – although interestingly, experience of a bad male minister doesn't elicit the same response!

3   They are: an easy tolerance, where anything goes, or an over-harsh response that does not allow for comfort or forgiveness. Group members can answer 'which do you tend towards' for themselves or for their church.

4   The motivation should be love. Remember Jesus' words in Revelation 3:19 and the words in Hebrews 12:7–13. Discipline should be designed to be redemptive, not to punish people or push them away from the church (Mt. 18:15).

5   Discipline should take consideration of the direction of a believer's life so the two should be treated differently. A new Christian will need patient discipleship rather than discipline.

6   The sword symbolises the word of God, both in terms of the Bible and Jesus himself. God's method for overcoming error is the truth of the gospel of Christ.

7   To Pergamum, Jesus promises some of the hidden manna – there was a Jewish tradition that when the Messiah came, he would bring with him a sample of the old manna given to the Israelites in the wilderness, a symbol of God's

faithfulness and provision. They were also promised a white stone. This may refer to the custom of giving a stone to a man at the end of a trial – white for not guilty. White stones were also used as admission tickets at festivals – the church from Pergamum will be guests at Christ's banquet for the faithful. The new name is almost certainly the name of Christ (3:12), 'secret' until eternity reveals the full nature of our renewed relationship with him.

The Thyatirans are promised authority, having been subject to the Romans for so long. They will be given the morning star – the Romans believed that Venus was the morning star and the emperor Domitian had compared himself to the morning star. Jesus is the true Morning Star (Rev. 22:16).

You could draw an outline of a person on a large sheet of paper, collect all the promises to those who overcome and write them around the edge.

8   Jesus knows where they live, even thought it is a hard place (2:13). He knows what they have done – he has not been distant but watching (2:13, 19). Jesus is the victorious one – with a sword and feet of bronze (2:12,18). He is in charge, not the emperor.

9   You could ask people if they have been in this situation themselves and have been encouraged by others – what worked and what didn't?

WORSHIP
Remind people of the symbolism of the white stones:

▶   They say show we are 'not guilty', forgiven by God
▶   They are a reminder that we invited to eat with Christ in his new kingdom

FOR FURTHER STUDY
Prophecy functions primarily in the worship of the church. Prophets predict, announce judgements, act symbolically and receive visions. Prophecy is a valuable gift which is to be evaluated by the congregation and delivered in an orderly way.

MATERIALS NEEDED

▶ A candle with some thorns to put around it, if possible, plus some small candles or nightlights

▶ Some information from an organisation that works on behalf of persecuted Christians, for information during the prayer time

FEEDBACK

Find out the stories of people's perseverance that inspired group members during the week.

TO SET THE SCENE

Allow people a few minutes to think back over their life. They may it find it easier to write in landmark events and then think about what happened around those times.

This session does not look at suffering in depth and you will need to be sensitive to group members' experiences. You could encourage people to follow up this session by talking and praying with friends, or choose to look more closely at suffering in a future housegroup session.

1   These two churches received no words of criticism, only praise and encouragement.

2   Sometimes this is to do with our life experience – perhaps we have never received much praise or encouragement from anyone. Sometimes it is because we have an incomplete picture of who God is – perhaps his judgement and holiness have been emphasised in the teaching we have heard, over his love and forgiveness.

3   We shouldn't feel that we have to sell Christianity or go overboard to persuade people to become Christians. It is the Holy Spirit who convicts. We do need to be real about the place of suffering in the Christian life, sharing our own story and talking about how God has helped us through difficult times.

4   164,000 Christians died for their faith in 1999. It can be hard to know how to respond to this, but there are organisations such as Release International and Voice of the Martyrs who provide information and suggestions for action. We

need to be informed and prayerful.

5   The church at Smyrna were promised the crown of life, and that those who overcome will not be hurt at all by the second death. The church at Philadelphia were told that those who had been their enemies would fall at their feet and acknowledge that Jesus had loved them. They would be kept from the hour of trial that was coming. Jesus promised to make those who overcame a pillar in his temple – they would never leave it and would have Jesus' name written on them.

6   As in some of the other letters, Jesus says that he knows about their situation – they are not alone and abandoned. Jesus encourages them, saying he will come soon and that they will be able to endure what is ahead.

7   Smyrna – they are afflicted and in poverty, yet Jesus calls them rich because they have what really matters, a strong faith in him. Philadelphia – though they are weak, Jesus sets before them an open door that no one can shut. Some people would maintain that success always follows faithfulness – that if a church is not prospering then they have not been faithful – but that does not tally with Jesus' words to Smyrna and Philadelphia.

9   Suffering is usually seen as something to be avoided; it carries with it feelings of punishment – people feel they must have done something wrong. Not everyone outside the church (or in it!) shares the same attitude to suffering so encourage several differing responses.

WORSHIP
Set a large candle in the centre of the room. Put some thorns around it from a rose bush or bramble, to represent Christ's suffering. Set some nightlights around it that people can light when they pray.

SESSION 8

MATERIALS NEEDED

▶ A large sheet of card, plus marker pens
▶ Small strips of card to write the 'barriers' on
▶ Blu-tack
▶ Chocolates

TO SET THE SCENE

Research has shown that most people become Christians through personal friendships – even those that make a commitment at an event are usually there because a friend has brought them along. Is this true for your group?

1   This is a slightly tongue-in-cheek activity. You could also talk about the evangelism that people have been involved in, as individuals or as part of the church, and times when people have been evangelised.

3   The Philadelphians lived in a very pagan society, where Christians were a seen as a minority of oddities. They had little strength and were facing real opposition.

4   On a large sheet of paper write down the possible areas of opportunity – the workplace, the school community, the street where you live, the area local to the church, sport or leisure activities and so on.

5   Encourage people to be honest – what stops them from sharing the gospel in these areas? Write down these barriers and reasons on small strips of card and stick them across the areas of life you have thought of.

6   Perhaps an openness to the gospel in a surprising place; several people having the same conviction about an opportunity; sometimes an invitation to get involved in an area; asking God to show you the open doors and then expecting an answer. It is not up to us to go it alone – we need the support, involvement and backing of the church.

7   It is not up to us to force our way in – it is the Holy Spirit who creates a hunger for God in people. So sometimes these reasons/barriers are real and show us that the time is not right – at other times we know that we tend to make up

excuses. Talk about how we can overcome shyness, embarrassment, or a lack of confidence about the gospel.

8   If most people do become Christians through friendships, that is a good place to start. How can we listen to people instead of talking at them?

WORSHIP
Pass round some chocolates as people share what they have learned. Pray that they will continue to feed on and be sustained by this study of Revelation.

As people pray about the areas of opportunity, encourage them to remove the barriers that you have stuck over the words. Ask God to make it clear which doors are open to you as individuals and as a church.

After the time of worship, you could talk about what you are going to do about these opportunities. How can you support each other?

FOR FURTHER STUDY
The early church was opposed by the Jewish leaders (Acts 4 & 6), the King (Acts 12) and a sorcerer (Acts 13), among others. The conversion of Paul brought a time of peace – is there someone significant that you need to pray for? It is probably unrealistic to say that they always met opposition with joy, but what is striking is their confidence in the gospel and their determination to keep preaching.

LETTERS TO THE CHURCHES

Quantity discount offer

To buy quantities of this workbook at a discount for use in study groups, please use the voucher below.

Get **Free** copies

- -

Name of Church representative: _____

Dear Retailer,
This completed voucher entitles the bearer to free additional copies of Spring Harvest Bible Workbooks. Please indicate the number of free copies supplied.

item	✔	cost
Buy 10 copies, get **1 free** (11 copies total)		£29.90
Buy 25 copies, get **5 free** (30 copies total)		£74.75
Buy 50 copies, get **15 free** (65 copies total)		£149.50

Vouchers will be credited less normal discount. Please return completed voucher to STL Customer Services, PO Box 300, Carlisle, CA3 0QS, by 31/01/2003

Name of Retailer: _____

STL A/C No: _____

Only one voucher to be used per customer. Voucher cannot be used in conjunction with any other offer. Voucher cannot be exchanged for anything other than the above product. No change will be given. Cash value 0.0001p   code: PATGENVOU

In case of difficulty in obtaining copies, please contact Spring Harvest direct at info@springharvest.org or on 01825 769111